Copyright Page

Pressure Reveals Path:
How God Uses What Breaks Us to Bring Us Home

© 2025 Steven Truitt
All rights reserved.

No part of this book may be reproduced, stored in a retrieval system, or transmitted in any form or by any means—electronic, mechanical, photocopying, recording, or otherwise—without the prior written permission of the publisher, except in the case of brief quotations used in reviews or scholarly works.

Published by
Light in the Darkness Publishing

Unless otherwise noted, Scripture quotations are taken from the Holy Bible, New International Version (NIV).
Copyright © 1973, 1978, 1984, 2011 by Biblica, Inc. Used by permission. All rights reserved worldwide.

All names, events, and personal stories are shared truthfully from the author's life. Some details may be altered for clarity or privacy without changing the substance of the events described.

This book is not intended to replace professional medical, psychological, or pastoral counseling. Readers are encouraged to seek appropriate guidance when needed.

Printed in the United States of America

First Edition

Dedication

This book is dedicated to my mother.

To a woman whose faith endured pressure,
whose prayers reached deeper than she knew,
and whose love became the fracture God used to guide me home.

You prayed that God would do whatever it took to bring your children back to Him.
He answered your prayer.

May my life honor your faith,
and may this book remind others that no prayer offered in love is ever wasted.

Anita Truitt, with me in 1972

Table of Contents

Introduction
Pressure Reveals Pathways

Chapter 1 — Five Miles Down
What happens beneath the surface matters more than what is seen

Chapter 2 — What Pressure Really Does
Why pressure reveals truth instead of destroying it

Chapter 3 — Comfort Is a Ceiling
How avoiding pressure limits growth and seals potential

Chapter 4 — The Myth of Being Broken Alone
Why fractures are meant to connect, not isolate

Chapter 5 — When Life Cracks the Rock
Loss, failure, grief, and the moments pressure becomes personal

Chapter 6 — Small Breaks That Lead Somewhere
Why no fracture is insignificant and how pathways are formed

Chapter 7 — The Path You Couldn't See
How pressure reveals direction that was hidden all along

Chapter 8 — Intertwined on Purpose
Why your fractures are meant to connect with others

Chapter 9 — The Pipe Always Leads Up
Why redemption has direction and God is the destination

Final Chapter — Where God Fractured Me
A call to listen to the small fractures before the large ones come

Written By: Steven Truitt

The Fracture That Led Me Home The Fracture That Led Me Home

Introduction

Most of us spend our lives trying to avoid pressure.

We organize our schedules to reduce it. We build routines to protect ourselves from it. We pray for its removal. Pressure is treated as the enemy of peace, the evidence that something has gone wrong.

But what if pressure is not the problem?

What if pressure is the process?

Deep beneath the surface of the earth, there are formations that hold tremendous value. They exist under immense weight, sealed tight by time and compression. Left alone, nothing moves. Everything remains intact—but inaccessible.

To release what is trapped, pressure must be applied.

Not to destroy the formation, but to fracture it. Those fractures spread outward, intersecting with others, forming pathways. Eventually, those pathways connect to the pipe—and what was buried five miles down begins its journey upward.

This book was born from that realization.

Pressure does not always destroy.
Sometimes, it reveals.

Throughout these pages, you will see pressure not as punishment, but as preparation. Fractures not as failure, but as formation. Brokenness not as the end of the story, but as the beginning of direction.

You will read about comfort—and why it often becomes a ceiling. About small breaks we ignore and large breaks we cannot. About isolation, connection, and the pathways formed when fractures intertwine. And ultimately, about God—not only present in the depth, but waiting at the surface.

This is not a book about avoiding pain.
It is a book about not wasting it.

You may recognize yourself somewhere in these chapters. In the pressure you did not choose. In the fractures you tried to seal. In the quiet sense that something deeper is happening beneath the surface of your life.

If so, this book is for you.

Because the pressure you are under may not be crushing you.
It may be guiding you home.

Chapter 1

Five Miles Down**

Most of what matters in life happens far below the surface.

We live in a world trained to measure what can be seen—results, appearances, outcomes, success, failure. We talk about what rises quickly and what collapses publicly. We notice what shines, what breaks loudly, and what draws attention. But the most consequential work often happens where no one is watching, in places hidden from view, under layers of weight and time.

Deep beneath the surface of the earth, far beyond sunlight and sound, there are formations that have existed long before any of us arrived. They are silent, compressed, and unseen. Nothing about them suggests movement. Nothing about them looks productive. And yet, they hold immense potential.

To reach them, you don't skim the ground. You go down.

Modern oil and gas wells routinely extend twenty-six to thirty thousand feet into the earth—over five miles deep. At that depth, there is no margin for guessing. Every decision must be precise. Every step is intentional. The pressures involved are immense, and the environment is unforgiving.

At five miles down, you cannot see where you are going.
You rely on what you know.

When a well reaches its target formation, the work is not finished—it is only beginning. The formation itself is dense and tight, locked in place by time and pressure. On its own, it will not release what it holds. Not because it lacks value, but because it has never been opened.

That is where pressure comes in.

Hydraulic fracturing works by applying controlled pressure into the rock—pressure strong enough to break it, but not destroy it. The goal is not collapse. The goal is connection. When pressure is applied, the rock fractures. Small cracks begin to form, often invisible at first. These fractures do not exist in isolation. They move outward, intersecting with other fractures, expanding through the formation.

What begins as a single break becomes a network.

Over time, thousands of tiny fractures connect to one another, forming a pathway back to the wellbore—the pipe that leads to the surface. And when that pathway is established, what was once trapped deep below can finally move upward.

The pressure does not eliminate the formation.
It reveals the way through it.

This is the part most people misunderstand.

Pressure is often assumed to be destructive. In life, we associate pressure with failure, collapse, or loss. We speak of being "under pressure" as though it is something to escape at all costs. Comfort is marketed as the ultimate goal, and relief is treated as the highest good.

But deep underground, pressure is not the enemy. It is the mechanism.

Without pressure, nothing moves.
Without pressure, the formation remains sealed.
Without pressure, what exists below never reaches the surface.

The same truth applies to us.

Much of what defines a person is not revealed in moments of ease, but in seasons of compression. Loss, disappointment, grief, failure, and uncertainty apply a kind of pressure that comfort never will. They force questions we would rather avoid. They expose limits we did not want to see. They break open assumptions we were sure would hold.

And yet, pressure does not create something foreign within us.
It exposes what was already there.

This is where the metaphor turns personal for every reader, regardless of background or belief.

Most people carry the quiet assumption that brokenness is proof of failure. That if something cracks, it means something went wrong. That fractures must be hidden, repaired quickly, or denied altogether. We learn early how to mask pain, manage appearances, and present a version of ourselves that looks intact.

But fractures are not the same as destruction.

In rock formations, fractures are not defects—they are features. They are the means by which connection becomes possible. A single fracture does little on its own. But when fractures intersect, something changes. They form channels. They create movement. They allow what was trapped to travel.

In life, our fractures often feel isolating. Shame convinces us that our pain separates us from others. Loss tells us we are alone. Failure whispers that we are uniquely broken. But fractures rarely exist in isolation. They run outward. They intersect with other stories, other wounds, other pressures.

This is where something unexpected happens.

What feels like personal breaking often becomes shared ground.

Grief connects to grief.
Failure recognizes failure.
Loss finds loss.

Suddenly, what once felt isolating becomes relational. Not because the pain disappears, but because it finds resonance. The fracture becomes a point of connection.

And connection changes everything.

In hydraulic fracturing, the goal is not to create chaos. It is to create a pathway. Every fracture is oriented toward a direction. Every break contributes to a larger network. Nothing is random. Nothing is wasted.

The pathway always leads back to the pipe.
And the pipe always leads upward.

This matters more than it may seem.

Life under pressure often feels directionless. When things break, it can feel as though everything is scattering outward, losing coherence, dissolving into fragments. But pressure, when applied within purpose, does not lead to disintegration—it leads to flow.

The fractures have a destination.

This is where faith enters the conversation—not as a slogan, but as a framework for meaning.

Scripture consistently describes God as a builder, a refiner, a redeemer—one who works with material as it is, not as we wish it were. The language of refining, pruning, shaping, and forming appears again and again. None of it happens without pressure. None of it happens without resistance.

Gold is refined under heat.
Stone is shaped under force.
Lives are transformed under weight.

The assumption that faith should eliminate pressure is not found in Scripture. Instead, faith reframes pressure. It assigns meaning to it. It insists that what feels like breaking may actually be preparation.

This does not make pain easy.
It makes it purposeful.

There is a difference.

Purpose does not remove suffering.
Purpose redeems it.

When pressure reveals fractures, it also reveals pathways. It shows where connection is possible.

It shows where healing can flow. It shows how individual breaks can become collective strength.

This is why comfort, when elevated as the highest goal, often becomes a ceiling. Comfort resists pressure. Comfort avoids fracture. Comfort keeps everything intact—but sealed. It preserves the formation, but prevents flow.

Nothing moves without pressure.

This is not a call to seek suffering or glorify pain. It is an invitation to stop interpreting pressure as failure. It is a reframing of what it means to be broken.

Broken does not mean useless.
Fractured does not mean finished.

In the formation, fractures are the very thing that allow value to be released. Without them, the resource remains trapped forever. Without them, the depth serves no purpose.

The same is true for the human heart.

Many people spend their lives trying to repair every crack before anyone sees it, unaware that those cracks may be the very places where connection, compassion, and calling emerge. We hide the fractures God intends to use. We seal what He is trying to open.

But pressure has a way of undoing that.

Pressure removes illusions.
Pressure exposes weakness.
Pressure reveals what is real.

And what is real is where transformation begins.

The pathway back to the surface is not built in one moment. It is formed over time, through many small fractures intersecting, aligning, and connecting. Each one matters. Each one contributes.

No fracture is insignificant.

This is why your story matters—not just the parts that look whole, but the places that cracked under weight. Those fractures may be closer to purpose than you realize.

The pressure did not destroy you.
It revealed the pathway.

And every pathway, when followed, leads upward.

Chapter 2

What Pressure Really Does**

Pressure is rarely the problem we think it is.

Most people assume pressure is destructive by nature. That it only crushes, overwhelms, or damages what it touches. In everyday language, pressure is something to escape, reduce, or relieve as quickly as possible. When pressure increases in life, we instinctively search for release—any outlet that promises comfort or control.

But pressure itself is neutral.
It does not decide the outcome.
It only reveals the condition of what it is applied to.

In engineering, pressure is never treated as an accident. It is calculated, anticipated, and directed. The question is never whether pressure will exist, but whether the system is prepared for it. Properly understood, pressure does not destroy strong systems—it exposes weak ones and activates purposeful ones.

This distinction matters.

In hydraulic fracturing, pressure is not applied randomly. It is measured in real time, adjusted constantly, and constrained within limits designed to work with the formation rather than against it. Too little pressure, and nothing happens. Too much, and damage occurs. But when pressure is applied within purpose, it accomplishes something precise.

It opens what was sealed.

This truth carries into life more directly than we may want to admit.

Pressure reveals alignment—or lack of it.
It exposes assumptions.
It tests foundations.

Comfort hides these things. Pressure does not.

When everything is easy, unresolved weaknesses remain buried. Relationships seem stable. Beliefs go unchallenged. Identity feels secure. But ease has a way of masking fragility. It delays reckoning. It preserves appearances.

Pressure accelerates truth.

When pressure enters a system—whether mechanical or human—it forces a response. Something must give. Something must move. Something must be confronted. Pressure does not invent problems; it reveals where the structure was already vulnerable.

This is why seasons of pressure often feel unfair. They do not introduce new issues so much as uncover old ones. Long-held fears surface.

Hidden resentments emerge. Fragile beliefs fracture. The pressure feels personal, but its work is diagnostic before it is transformative.

In the subsurface, rock formations exist under pressure constantly. The deeper the formation, the greater the pressure. That pressure alone does not cause failure. The rock has endured it for millennia. But when additional pressure is introduced—intentional pressure—the rock responds according to its internal structure.

Brittle rock fractures.
Ductile rock bends.
Weak points reveal themselves.

The response is not arbitrary. It is honest.

The same is true in human life. Pressure does not make us something we are not. It makes visible what has always been there. It shows us where we are rigid, where we are flexible, and where we are fragile.

This is uncomfortable knowledge.

We would prefer pressure to be random—something that happens to us rather than something that reveals us. But pressure has a way of stripping away illusions. It removes our ability to perform, to manage perceptions, or to maintain control.

Under pressure, pretending becomes exhausting. Under pressure, truth surfaces.

This is why pressure often feels threatening to identity. Many of us build our sense of self around stability—what we can manage, provide, endure, or predict. Pressure disrupts that narrative. It introduces uncertainty. It exposes dependence. It challenges autonomy.

But disruption is not destruction.

In fact, disruption is often the doorway to growth.

Consider how pressure functions in refinement. Metals are strengthened under stress. Diamonds are formed under immense compression. Muscles grow not through ease, but resistance. In each case, pressure is not the enemy of strength—it is the environment that produces it.

The problem is not pressure itself, but unmanaged pressure. Pressure without purpose leads to collapse. Pressure without direction leads to chaos. But pressure applied with intention leads to transformation.

This is where faith reframes the experience.

If pressure is random, then suffering is meaningless. But if pressure is permitted within purpose, then suffering becomes formative. This does not minimize pain. It dignifies it. It suggests that what feels like opposition may actually be participation in a larger process.

Scripture consistently presents God as one who works through pressure rather than around it. Refining fire, pruning shears, wilderness seasons, storms, and trials are not described as interruptions to spiritual growth, but as instruments of it.

This challenges modern assumptions about comfort.

Comfort promises preservation.
Pressure produces formation.

Comfort keeps things as they are. Pressure changes them.

This is why prolonged comfort often leads to stagnation. Without pressure, there is no reason to examine motives, no incentive to grow, and no urgency to depend on anything beyond oneself. Comfort creates the illusion of sufficiency.

Pressure dismantles that illusion.

When pressure increases, it forces a question: *What am I really anchored to?* What holds when the surface stability disappears? What remains when familiar structures fail?

These questions are not meant to condemn. They are meant to clarify.

In the subsurface, fractures do not form everywhere—only where stress exceeds strength. Those fractures reveal where movement is possible. They indicate where flow can occur. Without fractures, the formation remains isolated, regardless of its potential.

Isolation is the hidden danger of comfort.

Comfort isolates pain.
Pressure connects it.

Under pressure, fractures intersect. One crack meets another. Individual points of weakness link into networks. What was once sealed off becomes accessible. Movement becomes possible.

In life, pressure often does the same. Shared hardship creates connection. Mutual struggle builds empathy. Collective suffering dismantles hierarchy and exposes common humanity. Pressure reminds us that we are not alone—not because pain disappears, but because it becomes shared.

This is where purpose emerges.

The fractures formed under pressure are not endpoints; they are beginnings. They create pathways—channels through which healing, understanding, compassion, and redemption can flow. They turn isolated pain into collective strength.

But this only happens if the pressure is allowed to do its work.

Resisting pressure at all costs leads to brittleness. Avoiding discomfort leads to rigidity. Refusing to bend eventually leads to breaking. But accepting pressure as formative allows it to shape rather than shatter.

This is not passive acceptance. It is intentional trust.

Trust that pressure is not proof of abandonment.
Trust that breaking does not equal failure.
Trust that God works beneath the surface long before anything reaches the light.

The pathway back to the surface does not appear instantly. It is built gradually, fracture by fracture, connection by connection. Each response to pressure matters. Each decision under weight shapes the outcome.

Pressure asks a question of every life it touches:

Will you resist, or will you be formed?

The answer determines whether pressure becomes destructive or transformative.

By the time anything reaches the surface, the real work has already been done in the dark. The formation has been opened. The pathway has been established. Flow is now possible.

Pressure did not ruin the system.
It prepared it.

And what pressure prepares, it eventually releases.

Chapter 3

Comfort Is a Ceiling**

Comfort is rarely recognized as a limitation. More often, it is celebrated as a goal.

From an early age, we are trained—intentionally or not—to pursue ease. Stability, security, predictability, and convenience are presented as signs of success. If life becomes uncomfortable, the assumption is that something has gone wrong. Discomfort is treated as an interruption rather than an invitation.

But comfort, while not inherently wrong, has a quiet consequence.
It limits growth.

A ceiling is not something you usually notice while standing beneath it. It only becomes obvious when you try to rise. Comfort functions the same way. It creates a sense of containment. It defines the height to which we are willing to stretch, the risks we are willing to take, and the truths we are willing to confront.

Comfort does not stop life.
It stalls it.

In the subsurface, formations can remain intact for thousands of years. They hold potential, energy, and value, yet nothing moves. The rock is stable. Predictable. Safe. But sealed. Without intervention, without pressure, everything valuable remains locked away.

Comfort preserves the formation.
Pressure releases it.

This is not immediately intuitive, especially when applied to life. Comfort feels like peace. Pressure feels like threat. But peace and comfort are not the same thing. Peace can exist in pressure. Comfort cannot.

Comfort requires control.
Peace requires trust.

This distinction changes how we interpret difficulty. When comfort becomes the highest priority, pressure becomes the enemy. But when growth becomes the goal, pressure becomes the process.

One of the most subtle dangers of comfort is how reasonable it feels. Comfort rarely announces itself as compromise. It presents itself as wisdom. As prudence. As responsibility. It whispers, *Why risk what you already have?* It suggests that staying put is safer than stepping forward, that maintaining stability is better than pursuing calling.

Over time, this mindset reshapes desire. We stop asking what we were made for and start asking what we can manage. We exchange purpose for predictability. We lower expectations—not because we lack potential, but because potential demands pressure.

Comfort is appealing because it minimizes exposure.
Pressure demands vulnerability.

In hydraulic operations, a well that never experiences sufficient pressure will never produce. It may look complete from the surface. The casing is set. The infrastructure is in place. Everything appears finished. But without pressure, the well is functionally dormant.

Appearance without flow is not success.

This is where comfort becomes deceptive. A life can look full from the outside while remaining sealed on the inside. Busy schedules, polished routines, and managed responsibilities can create the impression of vitality, even while something essential remains untapped.

Comfort excels at maintaining appearances.
Pressure exposes reality.

This exposure is uncomfortable precisely because it challenges identity. Many people build their sense of self around what they can keep intact.

Pressure threatens that stability. It introduces uncertainty. It demands adaptation. It forces dependence.

But identity that cannot survive pressure is fragile.

When comfort dominates, we often begin to confuse safety with faithfulness. We assume that if a path feels risky, it must be wrong. If a decision produces anxiety, it must be avoided. But discomfort is not a reliable indicator of misalignment. Often, it is a sign of growth.

Growth stretches capacity.
Stretching feels like strain.

Every meaningful expansion requires leaving something familiar. Muscles tear before they strengthen. Skills develop through repetition and failure. Wisdom forms through experience, not avoidance. In every domain, growth requires pressure.

Spiritual growth is no exception.

Scripture does not present comfort as the primary environment for transformation. Again and again, growth occurs in deserts, storms, prisons, wildernesses, and waiting seasons. These are not accidents of history. They are contexts of formation.

Comfort rarely asks us to change.
Pressure insists on it.

This is why prolonged comfort often leads to complacency. Over time, we stop questioning assumptions. We stop listening deeply. We stop examining motives. Comfort dulls urgency. It convinces us there will always be time later—for obedience, for reconciliation, for courage.

Pressure collapses that illusion.

Under pressure, time feels compressed. Decisions matter. Priorities clarify. What once felt optional becomes essential. Pressure sharpens focus. It strips away distractions and forces attention toward what truly matters.

This clarity is one of pressure's greatest gifts.

Yet many people spend their lives insulating themselves against it. We design routines, habits, and systems specifically to avoid discomfort. We buffer schedules, limit exposure, and control environments. Over time, we become highly efficient at managing life—but inefficient at living it.

Comfort rewards maintenance.
Pressure produces movement.

In subsurface engineering, a formation that remains unfractured is isolated—not just from the surface, but from other formations. Pressure creates connection. It opens channels. It allows interaction. Comfort seals boundaries.

Isolation is one of comfort's hidden costs.

A comfortable life can become a solitary one—not physically, but emotionally and spiritually. Without pressure, we rarely reveal weakness. Without weakness, intimacy remains shallow. Without intimacy, community becomes transactional.

Pressure, by contrast, has a way of leveling hierarchy. It reminds us of shared limits. It exposes common need. It invites honesty. Under pressure, people stop performing and start relating.

This is why some of the deepest connections form during the hardest seasons. Shared struggle creates bonds that comfort never can. Pressure opens pathways not only within us, but between us.

Still, comfort resists this truth. It argues for containment. It suggests that exposure is dangerous. That vulnerability should be limited. That strength is proven by self-sufficiency.

But self-sufficiency is not strength.
It is isolation.

Pressure reveals dependence—not as weakness, but as design. No formation produces on its own. No fracture functions alone. Everything valuable flows through connection.

This principle applies universally.

When comfort becomes the ceiling, we stop reaching upward. We stop exploring depth. We stop asking difficult questions. We remain within known limits—not because God has constrained us, but because we have constrained ourselves.

Ceilings are self-reinforcing. The longer we live beneath them, the more normal they feel. We forget there is anything above. We forget that ceilings are meant to be broken through, not settled under.

Pressure breaks ceilings.

It does so by forcing movement. By introducing friction. By challenging the status quo. Pressure disrupts equilibrium—and equilibrium, while stable, is rarely transformative.

Transformation requires imbalance.
Growth requires disruption.

This is uncomfortable language because it challenges deeply held assumptions about what a good life looks like. We are conditioned to equate goodness with ease. But a good life is not necessarily an easy one. It is a meaningful one.

Meaning is forged, not preserved.

This is why comfort, when elevated to an ultimate goal, often leads to regret. Not because comfort is bad, but because it crowds out calling. Over time, we look back not on what we protected, but on what we failed to pursue.

Pressure confronts this hesitation directly.

When pressure enters life, it asks uncomfortable questions:

What matters most?
What are you trusting in?
What are you avoiding?
What are you willing to lose in order to gain?

Comfort avoids these questions. Pressure demands answers.

This demand can feel cruel. It can feel unfair. But it is also clarifying. Pressure accelerates maturity. It compresses growth that might otherwise take decades.

In engineering terms, pressure increases efficiency.

A formation that might never produce under natural conditions can be activated through intentional pressure. The same is true in life. Potential that might remain dormant indefinitely can be released through seasons of strain.

This does not mean pressure is always desirable. But it is often necessary.

The danger is not experiencing pressure.
The danger is wasting it.

When pressure arrives, we can respond in one of two ways: resistance or formation. Resistance fights pressure, resents it, and seeks escape. Formation submits to pressure, learns from it, and allows it to shape.

Resistance hardens.
Formation transforms.

Comfort encourages resistance. It frames pressure as interruption. Formation reframes pressure as instruction.

This shift changes everything.

When comfort is no longer the ceiling, growth becomes possible. We begin to interpret difficulty differently. We stop asking, *How do I get out of this?* and start asking, *What is this producing?*

This is not passive endurance. It is active engagement. It is choosing to learn rather than merely survive. It is trusting that pressure has direction—even when the destination is unclear.

In subsurface operations, the fractures do not know the surface exists. They simply respond to pressure. They connect. They move. They align. Eventually, flow happens.

Transformation often works the same way.

We do not always see where the pathway leads. We simply respond faithfully to pressure. We remain open. We allow connection. We resist the urge to seal ourselves off.

Over time, what once felt like confinement becomes conduit.

Comfort would have preserved the formation. Pressure creates the pathway.

This is why comfort must be recognized for what it is: a ceiling, not a destination. A temporary shelter, not a permanent home. Comfort is useful—but dangerous when it becomes ultimate.

The goal is not discomfort for its own sake.
The goal is movement toward purpose.

Pressure moves us.
Comfort keeps us still.

When the ceiling breaks, the sky opens.

And what waits above is worth the strain.

Chapter 4

The Myth of Being Broken Alone**

One of the most powerful lies we tell ourselves in moments of pain is that our suffering is unique.

Not unique in its details—everyone knows others have struggled—but unique in its isolation. We believe that while others may have experienced hardship, *this* fracture, *this* failure, *this* grief belongs to us alone. It feels personal, private, and separating. Pain convinces us that we are the exception, the outlier, the one who does not fit neatly into the stories of healing and restoration we see around us.

This belief does not arrive loudly.
It settles quietly.

It whispers that others would not understand.
It suggests that our struggle is inconvenient, embarrassing, or burdensome.
It convinces us that silence is safer than exposure.

And so we withdraw.

Isolation is rarely chosen outright. It is accumulated through small decisions—hesitations to speak, instincts to minimize, habits of self-protection. Over time, what began as self-preservation becomes separation. We remain physically present but emotionally sealed. Surrounded, yet alone.

But isolation is not the natural outcome of brokenness.
It is the result of believing a myth.

In the subsurface, fractures do not exist in isolation. A single fracture does little on its own. It may open slightly, but without connection it remains insignificant. The power of fracturing is not found in individual breaks, but in networks. Fractures intersect. They converge. They create pathways that none could form alone.

Brokenness behaves the same way.

When pain is isolated, it stagnates. When it is shared, it moves. Healing does not begin when fractures disappear; it begins when they connect.

This truth confronts a deep cultural instinct. We are trained to hide weakness, to present strength, to manage perception. Vulnerability is often framed as risk rather than necessity. We learn to believe that revealing fracture diminishes value.

But in reality, concealment diminishes connection.

The myth of being broken alone thrives in secrecy. It depends on comparison. We look at others' surfaces and assume they are whole, forgetting that surfaces rarely reveal what lies beneath. We compare our hidden fractures to others' visible stability and conclude that we are uniquely deficient.

This comparison is deeply misleading.

Every life carries fractures. Some are dramatic and visible. Others are quiet and concealed. Loss, rejection, shame, fear, disappointment, regret—these experiences are not rare anomalies. They are universal. What differs is not whether fractures exist, but whether they are acknowledged.

Pressure has a way of exposing this shared reality.

Under pressure, the illusion of self-sufficiency cracks. People reveal limits. Emotions surface. Defenses weaken. What once felt isolating begins to look familiar. We recognize ourselves in others' stories—not because the details match, but because the emotions do.

Pain has a common language.

This recognition can be unsettling. It challenges the narrative that we are alone. It disrupts the protective distance we have maintained. But it also opens the possibility of connection.

Connection requires exposure.
Exposure requires courage.

In geology, fractures intersect not because they seek each other, but because they respond to the same pressure. Shared pressure creates shared pathways. In life, shared experiences of strain often do the same. People who have endured similar pressures find each other—not intentionally at first, but naturally.

Grief recognizes grief.
Failure recognizes failure.
Fear recognizes fear.

These recognitions form the basis of empathy. Empathy is not sympathy from a distance; it is understanding born of shared fracture. It does not require identical stories. It requires honest ones.

This is why communities formed around shared hardship often feel deeper than those formed around shared success. Success can be celebrated at a distance. Pain demands proximity.

Yet many resist this proximity. We fear that sharing fracture will define us, limit us, or burden others. We worry that exposure will lead to rejection rather than connection.

Sometimes that fear is reinforced by experience. Not every response to vulnerability is gracious. Not every listener is safe. But isolation guarantees disconnection. It ensures that pain remains sealed.

Fractures that never connect never become pathways.

This is where the myth does its greatest damage. It convinces us that silence is strength and that endurance must be solitary. But endurance was never meant to be a solo act. Even the strongest materials distribute stress. They rely on structure. They depend on support.

Human beings are no different.

When fractures connect, something remarkable happens. Pain begins to move. It no longer circulates endlessly within a closed system. It flows outward, meeting understanding, compassion, and shared resilience. This movement does not erase pain, but it transforms its role.

Pain becomes a conduit rather than a cage.

This transformation often begins with language. Naming what hurts. Acknowledging what broke. Speaking what was previously hidden. These acts feel risky because they challenge control. Once spoken, pain can no longer be managed privately.

But unspoken pain is not neutral. It accumulates. It distorts perception. It isolates.

Connection interrupts this accumulation.

In the subsurface, when fractures connect to the wellbore, flow becomes possible. What was trapped begins to move toward the surface. In life, when fractures connect to community, healing begins to move toward visibility. What was hidden begins to be expressed.

This does not mean everyone must share everything with everyone. Discernment matters. Boundaries matter. But connection matters too.

The myth of being broken alone collapses when we recognize that our fractures are not aberrations—they are points of intersection. They are places where our story overlaps with others. They are invitations to relationship.

This recognition reframes brokenness.

Brokenness is not the absence of strength.
It is the context for shared strength.

Strength that stands alone eventually fractures under weight. Strength that is shared distributes pressure. It endures.

This is why vulnerability, when met with compassion, produces resilience. It creates networks of support. It builds pathways for mutual encouragement. It reminds us that we are not designed to carry everything by ourselves.

Pressure exposes fractures.
Connection redeems them.

But this redemption requires a shift in perspective. We must stop interpreting fracture as failure and start recognizing it as formation. We must stop hiding what hurts and start discerning where it might connect.

This shift does not happen instantly. It requires trust. It requires patience. It requires courage. But it begins with a simple acknowledgment: *I am not alone in this.*

Once that truth takes root, isolation loses its grip.

Communities built on shared fracture are not weak. They are honest. They do not deny pain; they integrate it. They create space for lament and hope to coexist. They allow people to be whole— not because they are unbroken, but because they are connected.

This kind of community cannot be manufactured. It emerges organically where people allow fractures to intersect. It grows slowly, through shared stories, mutual listening, and sustained presence.

It is fragile at first, like newly formed fractures. But over time, as connections deepen, it becomes resilient. It carries weight.

The myth of being broken alone tells us that fracture disqualifies us from belonging. The truth is the opposite. Fracture is often the doorway to belonging.

Belonging is not based on perfection.
It is built through honesty.

This honesty transforms how we see others. When we recognize our own fractures, we become less judgmental of others'. We listen more carefully. We respond more gently. We understand that strength and weakness are not opposites, but companions.

Pressure equalizes.
Connection humanizes.

In this way, fractures do more than heal individuals—they shape communities. They create cultures of empathy. They foster environments where growth is possible because pretense is unnecessary.

This is not sentimental idealism. It is practical wisdom. Systems that allow stress to be shared last longer. Structures that distribute weight endure. Lives that connect fracture to relationship sustain pressure.

The alternative is isolation, and isolation is unsustainable.

When fractures remain unconnected, pressure concentrates. Stress accumulates. Eventually, something fails. The failure may be emotional, relational, spiritual, or physical. But it is rarely sudden. It is the predictable result of carrying too much alone.

Connection relieves pressure by redistributing it.

This is why the myth of being broken alone must be dismantled. Not because pain is easy to share, but because it is too heavy to carry in isolation.

When fractures connect, pathways form. When pathways form, movement begins. When movement begins, healing becomes possible.

This is the quiet miracle hidden within brokenness.

You are not the only one who has cracked under pressure.
You are not the only one who has felt overwhelmed.
You are not the only one who has questioned your strength.

Your fracture is not a sentence.
It is an intersection.

And intersections are where journeys change direction.

Chapter 5

When Life Cracks the Rock**

Pressure is theoretical until it becomes personal.

We can talk about pressure in abstract terms—forces, systems, environments—but eventually pressure shows up with a name. It arrives as a phone call you were not prepared to receive. A diagnosis that reorders your future. A loss that leaves silence where presence once lived. A failure that exposes limits you did not know you had. A betrayal that fractures trust. A moment when life no longer fits the shape you expected it to take.

This is when the metaphor turns real.

Before that moment, pressure is something that happens to *others*. After it, pressure becomes the air you breathe. It presses in from every side. It changes how you think, how you feel, how you see the world. Familiar ground no longer feels stable. What once felt solid begins to shift.

Life cracks the rock.

These cracks are rarely clean. They do not follow neat lines. They cut across assumptions, plans, and identities. They fracture not only circumstances, but meaning. We begin to ask questions we never needed to ask before: *Why did this happen? What now? Who am I if this doesn't change?*

These questions are not signs of weakness. They are signs that pressure has reached depth.

In geology, fractures form when stress exceeds strength. But strength is not a moral quality; it is a structural one. A rock does not fail because it is bad. It fractures because it is finite. The same is true of people. We do not crack because we are deficient. We crack because we are human.

Loss exposes this finiteness most clearly.

Grief has a unique pressure. It compresses time. Days stretch and collapse unpredictably. The world continues moving while something inside stops. Grief fractures routines, language, and expectations. It disrupts the illusion that life can be managed through planning alone.

Grief also isolates—at least initially. Others may offer sympathy, but the experience itself feels singular. No one else is carrying *this* absence. No one else feels *this* weight. The fracture feels deeply personal.

Failure creates a different kind of crack.

Failure fractures identity. It challenges narratives we have told ourselves about competence, calling, and worth. It exposes gaps between intention and outcome. It forces confrontation with limitation. Failure does not just disappoint; it destabilizes.

For many, failure feels more threatening than loss because it invites blame—internal or external. Loss can be mourned. Failure feels judged. It carries shame, and shame thrives in secrecy.

Then there is betrayal.

Betrayal fractures trust, which is foundational to relationship. When trust breaks, it reshapes how we interpret the world. We become cautious. Guarded. Alert for threat. Betrayal does not just wound one relationship; it recalibrates our sense of safety.

And there are quieter cracks.

Chronic disappointment. Unanswered prayers. Long seasons of waiting. Persistent anxiety. Unfulfilled hopes. These pressures do not arrive dramatically. They accumulate. Over time, they weaken the structure from within. The fracture may not be obvious at first, but it is no less real.

All of these experiences share something in common: they apply pressure beyond what we expected to carry.

When that happens, the instinctive response is resistance. We try to hold everything together. We double down on control. We attempt to seal the crack before it spreads. We tell ourselves to be strong, to move on, to push through.

Sometimes this works—for a while.

But unacknowledged fractures do not heal. They simply shift. Pressure that cannot be released finds other outlets. Emotional strain becomes physical. Spiritual confusion becomes relational distance. Suppressed grief becomes bitterness. Unprocessed failure becomes fear of risk.

The rock does not forget where it cracked.

This is why the moment life cracks the rock is so significant. It marks a transition. What happens next determines whether the fracture becomes destructive or transformative.

In subsurface operations, fractures are not feared; they are monitored. Engineers pay close attention to where fractures form, how they propagate, and what they connect to. A fracture is information. It reveals stress patterns. It indicates pathways. It shows where movement is possible.

In life, fractures provide similar information—if we are willing to pay attention.

What breaks often reveals what mattered.
What cracks often exposes what was carrying too much weight.

What fails often highlights what was never meant to be self-sustaining.

This does not make the experience easier. But it does make it meaningful.

When life cracks the rock, it interrupts false narratives. It dismantles the illusion of invulnerability. It confronts us with our dependence—not as a flaw, but as a reality. We were never meant to be unbreakable. We were meant to be connected.

This realization is often resisted because it feels like loss of control. But control was always partial. Pressure reveals that truth.

The crack is not the end of the story.
It is the beginning of a new chapter.

This is where perspective matters.

If we interpret cracks as proof of failure, we will rush to conceal them. We will isolate. We will harden. But if we interpret cracks as points of access—places where something new can enter or emerge—we respond differently.

We become curious instead of defensive.
We become honest instead of performative.
We become open instead of sealed.

This openness is not immediate. It takes time. It often begins with grief—grief not only for what was lost, but for what we thought life would be. Expectations die slowly. Identity reshapes gradually. Pressure does not resolve on our timeline.

But something important happens in the waiting.

As cracks remain exposed, they begin to intersect with others. Shared loss meets shared loss. Shared failure meets shared failure. What once felt isolating becomes relational. The fracture becomes a meeting place.

This is where healing begins—not when the crack disappears, but when it connects.

Connection does not eliminate pain. It changes its direction. Pain no longer circulates endlessly within us; it moves outward. It becomes shared, understood, and carried together.

In the formation, once fractures connect, flow begins—not instantly, but inevitably. What was trapped starts to move. Pressure finds release. Energy is redirected.

In life, when cracks connect to meaning, community, and purpose, something similar happens. The pain does not vanish, but it is no longer wasted. It begins to serve.

This is perhaps the hardest truth to accept: that some cracks are necessary.

Not because pain is good, but because growth often requires disruption. The rock does not open without fracture. Potential does not release without pressure. New pathways do not form without breaking old seals.

This truth confronts our desire for preservation. We want growth without loss, transformation without disruption, healing without pain. But life does not work that way.

The good news is not that cracks are avoidable. The good news is that cracks are not final.

They are formative.

When life cracks the rock, it exposes depth we did not know existed. It reveals capacity we did not know we needed. It opens us to dependence, humility, and compassion. It reshapes how we relate to others and to ourselves.

It also clarifies what matters.

Pressure strips away non-essentials. It reveals priorities. It forces alignment. What once seemed important fades. What truly matters comes into focus. This clarity, though costly, is valuable.

Many people look back on the most painful seasons of their lives and recognize them as turning points—not because they enjoyed the pain, but because those seasons changed direction. They redirected energy. They reshaped purpose. They opened pathways that comfort never would have.

This does not mean every crack leads to growth automatically. Formation is not guaranteed. It is possible to harden instead of open, to isolate instead of connect, to resent instead of reflect.

But when cracks are met with honesty and openness, they become gateways.

Gateways to empathy.
Gateways to humility.
Gateways to purpose.

Life cracks the rock to reveal what lies beneath.

What lies beneath is not weakness alone. It is depth. It is capacity. It is potential that could not surface any other way.

The crack is not the conclusion.
It is the access point.

And once access exists, pressure can do its work—not to destroy, but to direct.

The pathway is forming, even if you cannot see it yet.

Chapter 6

Small Breaks That Lead Somewhere**

Not every break feels significant.

Some fractures arrive quietly. They do not announce themselves with catastrophe or crisis. They slip into life as disappointments that never quite resolve, tensions that linger beneath the surface, questions that remain unanswered. These small breaks are easy to dismiss. Compared to loss or failure, they seem manageable—hardly worth naming.

But in the subsurface, small fractures are never ignored.

In fact, they are essential.

Large fractures rarely form all at once. They emerge from clusters of microfractures—tiny breaks that appear insignificant in isolation but powerful in combination. Each one alters stress distribution. Each one redirects pressure. Each one contributes to a larger pattern of movement.

Pathways are not sudden inventions.
They are cumulative constructions.

This is where many misunderstand formation—both geological and personal. We assume change requires dramatic moments, decisive events, clear turning points. But more often, transformation is shaped by accumulation. Small responses repeated over time. Small decisions under pressure. Small cracks allowed to remain open instead of sealed shut.

These are the breaks that lead somewhere.

In life, small fractures often take the form of unmet expectations. A conversation that never happened. A prayer that seemed unanswered. A role that did not unfold as hoped. A relationship that slowly drifted instead of suddenly ending. These experiences may not feel life-altering, but they exert pressure nonetheless.

Pressure accumulates quietly.

Left unacknowledged, small fractures can feel like background noise—persistent but tolerable. Yet over time, they change internal structure. They reshape how we trust, how we hope, how we risk. They influence how we respond when larger pressures arrive.

Small breaks prepare the formation.

This preparation can work in two directions.

When small fractures are denied, ignored, or suppressed, they harden the system. Pressure builds without release. Stress concentrates. Eventually, when pressure exceeds capacity, the result is often catastrophic—an abrupt failure that feels disproportionate to the immediate cause.

But when small fractures are acknowledged and allowed to connect, they create flexibility. They distribute stress. They form early pathways that guide future pressure. When larger fractures arrive, the system is already prepared to respond.

The difference is not the presence of pressure.
It is the presence of pathways.

This truth reframes how we interpret the everyday disappointments of life. What if those moments were not merely inconveniences, but formative fractures? What if they were shaping internal channels—quietly preparing us for pressures we have not yet encountered?

This perspective does not minimize pain. It assigns it meaning.

In hydraulic operations, fracture stages are carefully spaced. Each stage builds upon the previous one. Engineers understand that no single stage produces on its own. Production comes from the collective effect of many stages working together.

No fracture stands alone.
No stage is wasted.

In the same way, no experience is isolated. What happens early influences what happens later. Small disappointments shape resilience. Minor failures teach adaptability. Quiet seasons of waiting cultivate patience. These experiences do not feel productive, but they are preparatory.

Preparation is rarely dramatic.

Most of life's formation happens unnoticed, beneath the surface, where no one applauds progress and no metrics measure growth. We become someone long before we do something.

Small breaks contribute to that becoming.

They teach us how to live with tension.
They teach us how to endure ambiguity.
They teach us how to hold hope without certainty.

These lessons are not glamorous, but they are essential.

The temptation, of course, is to seal small fractures quickly. To resolve tension prematurely. To distract ourselves from discomfort. To move on without reflection. This impulse is understandable. Small pain feels unnecessary. Why linger when we can avoid?

But avoidance often delays formation.

When small fractures are sealed, pressure does not disappear—it reroutes. It finds other weaknesses. It expresses itself in anxiety, irritability, cynicism, or disengagement. What could have become a pathway becomes a pressure point.

Acknowledgment changes that dynamic.

Acknowledgment does not mean overanalyzing every disappointment. It means allowing experiences to register honestly. It means giving language to what hurts, even when it feels minor. It means resisting the urge to rush resolution.

This kind of honesty creates internal space.

In geology, fractures propagate along lines of weakness. These weaknesses are not defects; they are natural features of the rock. Grain boundaries, bedding planes, and existing microfractures guide how pressure moves.

Human lives have similar features. Personal history, temperament, relationships, and beliefs shape how pressure is experienced. Small breaks often follow these existing lines—not to exploit them, but to open them.

What feels like vulnerability is often alignment.

When small fractures connect along these lines, they form coherent pathways. They create continuity. They give pressure direction.

Direction is what distinguishes formation from chaos.

Without direction, pressure scatters energy. With direction, pressure focuses it. Small fractures help establish that direction.

This is why reflection matters. Reflection allows us to see patterns. It helps us recognize how small experiences are shaping larger trajectories. It reveals where pressure is consistently applied and where responses are forming.

Over time, these responses become habits.

Habits of honesty.
Habits of dependence.
Habits of humility.
Habits of courage.

Or, if left unattended, habits of avoidance.
Habits of self-protection.
Habits of disengagement.

Small fractures influence which habits take root.

This influence becomes evident when larger pressures arrive. People who have learned to respond honestly to small breaks are more likely to remain open under greater strain. They are familiar with fracture. They recognize it as part of the process rather than a threat to identity.

By contrast, those who have avoided small discomforts often experience larger pressures as overwhelming. Without existing pathways, pressure concentrates. The response becomes defensive. Isolation increases. Growth stalls.

This is not a moral judgment. It is a structural reality.

Structures that adapt gradually withstand stress better than those that resist change until forced.

The same principle applies to lives.

Small breaks also shape empathy. Those who have paid attention to minor disappointments often recognize them in others. They listen differently. They respond with patience. They understand that pain does not need to be catastrophic to be real.

This sensitivity creates connection.

Connection further strengthens pathways.

In the subsurface, once fractures intersect, they reinforce one another. Flow increases. Pressure decreases. Stability improves. The system becomes more resilient.

Resilience is not the absence of fracture.
It is the presence of connection.

This redefines strength.

Strength is not remaining unbroken.
Strength is remaining open.

Open to learning.
Open to connection.
Open to formation.

Small breaks cultivate this openness.

They remind us that we are finite. That expectations are provisional. That plans evolve. That identity is shaped over time, not fixed in place.

This reminder is uncomfortable, but it is also liberating.

When we stop demanding perfection from ourselves, we stop interpreting every crack as failure. We become more patient with process. We allow growth to unfold gradually.

Gradual growth is sustainable growth.

In hydraulic fracturing, production does not peak immediately. It builds over time as pathways stabilize and flow increases. Early stages may appear unremarkable. But their contribution becomes clear later, when the system reaches maturity.

The same is true in life.

Many of the most meaningful outcomes are the result of years of small, faithful responses to pressure. Moments that felt insignificant at the time later reveal themselves as essential.

This retrospective clarity does not negate the difficulty of the moment. But it reframes it.

Small breaks are not detours.
They are directions.

They point us toward depth, toward connection, toward purpose. They prepare us to carry greater weight without collapsing. They teach us how to live honestly within limitation.

This does not mean seeking out fracture. It means not wasting it.

When small breaks appear, the invitation is not to fix them immediately, but to listen. To ask what they reveal. To notice where they might connect. To remain open to what they are shaping.

This posture transforms everyday life.

Disappointment becomes instruction.
Delay becomes formation.
Tension becomes direction.

None of this is visible from the surface. It happens quietly, beneath awareness, under pressure.

But over time, pathways form.

When enough small fractures connect, movement begins. Flow increases. What was once trapped finds release. The surface eventually reflects what has been happening in secret all along.

Growth becomes visible because formation has been faithful.

Small breaks do not announce where they lead. They simply invite response.

And those responses, accumulated over time, determine whether pressure becomes destructive or directional.

Every pathway begins somewhere.
Most begin small.

Chapter 7

The Path You Couldn't See**

Most pathways are invisible until they are already in use.

From the surface, the earth looks solid—unchanging, stable, inert. There is no obvious indication of the networks that exist below, no hint of the channels that allow movement from depth to light. What appears still often contains tremendous activity hidden from view.

Life is similar.

We expect direction to be obvious. We want clarity before commitment, certainty before movement. We look for signs that confirm the path before we take the step. But formation rarely works that way. The path often appears only after pressure has done its work—after fractures have formed, after connections have been made, after movement has already begun.

This is one of the most disorienting aspects of pressure: it demands response before explanation.

When pressure increases, we often ask for a map. We want to know where this season is going, how long it will last, and what it will produce. We want assurance that the pain is purposeful. But pressure does not arrive with instructions. It arrives with demand.

The demand is simple and difficult at the same time: *respond honestly.*

Honesty under pressure is what reveals the path.

In the subsurface, pathways are not carved in advance. They are revealed through stress. Pressure exploits lines of weakness, not to exploit them, but to open them. The path exists potentially within the formation long before it becomes functional. Pressure activates it.

This distinction matters.

The path is not invented by pressure.
It is uncovered by it.

Many people assume that pressure forces them into something new and unwanted. But more often, pressure exposes what has been present but unused. Gifts long ignored. Convictions long deferred. Questions long avoided. Pressure does not create these things—it brings them to the surface.

This can feel threatening because it removes the option of delay.

Comfort allows postponement.
Pressure requires decision.

Under pressure, neutrality disappears. We cannot remain passive. Something must move. Something must change. The fracture demands response. And in responding, direction begins to emerge.

Direction is not the same as certainty.

Direction is orientation. It is movement with intention, even when the destination remains unclear. In formation, fractures do not know the surface exists. They simply respond to pressure and alignment. Over time, those responses converge into a pathway.

In life, direction often emerges the same way. We do not see the whole road. We respond to what is in front of us—honestly, faithfully, imperfectly. We make small decisions under pressure. We choose openness over isolation, courage over avoidance, truth over performance.

Those choices align fractures.

Alignment is what turns breaking into pathway.

Without alignment, fractures scatter. With alignment, they converge. The difference is not intensity of pressure, but orientation of response.

This is why two people can experience similar pressure and emerge in very different places. The pressure may be the same, but the response is not. One resists, seals, and isolates. The other opens, connects, and adapts. Over time, their internal structures diverge.

The path is not imposed.
It is formed.

This formation often feels backward. We want the outcome before the obedience. We want clarity before trust. But trust is what creates clarity—not the other way around.

This truth is difficult to accept because it confronts our desire for control. We want to manage outcomes. We want to minimize risk. We want assurance that our response will lead somewhere good.

Pressure offers no such guarantee.

What it offers instead is opportunity.

Opportunity to respond differently than before.
Opportunity to choose openness over self-protection.
Opportunity to allow fractures to connect rather than remain isolated.

These opportunities are easy to miss because they are subtle. They appear as invitations rather than commands. A conversation you could avoid—or enter honestly. A habit you could maintain—or examine. A fear you could suppress—or acknowledge.

These moments feel small, but they are directional.

Direction is shaped through consistency, not intensity.

One honest conversation does not create a pathway. Repeated honesty does. One courageous choice does not change a life. Sustained courage does. The path emerges through accumulation.

This accumulation happens beneath awareness. We rarely notice it in real time. We only recognize it later, when we realize that we are no longer where we started.

This realization can be surprising. We look back and see coherence where there once felt like chaos. We recognize how one decision led to another, how one connection opened the door to another, how one fracture intersected with another.

The path was forming all along.

This retrospective clarity does not mean the journey was easy. It means it was formative. The difficulty was not wasted. The pressure was not random. The fractures were not meaningless.

Meaning emerged through movement.

Movement requires trust—not in outcomes, but in process.

Trust that responding honestly matters even when results are unclear.
Trust that connection is safer than isolation, even when vulnerability feels risky.
Trust that pressure is not proof of abandonment, but invitation to formation.

This trust is rarely dramatic. It is practiced quietly, in ordinary moments, under ordinary strain.

The path you couldn't see becomes visible only after you start walking it.

This is why waiting for certainty often leads to stagnation. Certainty rarely precedes movement. It follows it. We discover what we believe by how we act under pressure.

Pressure clarifies belief.

When pressure increases, our true priorities surface. What we protect reveals what we value. What we pursue reveals what we trust. What we avoid reveals what we fear.

These revelations are uncomfortable, but they are honest.

Honesty is the foundation of direction.

Without honesty, movement becomes reactionary. We respond impulsively, driven by fear or comfort rather than intention. The result is scattered fracture—movement without coherence.

But with honesty, responses align. We begin to recognize patterns. We see where pressure consistently pushes. We notice recurring invitations. We discern where connection brings life and where isolation drains it.

Discernment grows through attention.

Attention requires slowing down enough to notice what pressure is revealing. This does not mean disengaging from responsibility. It means engaging more deeply with reality. It means asking better questions.

Not *How do I escape this?*
But *What is this shaping?*

Not *Why is this happening to me?*
But *What is this inviting me into?*

These questions shift posture from resistance to participation.

Participation changes everything.

When we participate in formation, we stop viewing ourselves as passive recipients of pressure and start recognizing our role in response. We cannot control the pressure, but we can choose how we respond to it.

Response is where agency lives.

This agency does not eliminate dependence. It deepens it. We become aware of our limits and our need for support. We seek connection rather than isolation. We allow others to carry weight with us.

This shared weight-bearing strengthens pathways.

In the subsurface, flow increases as pathways stabilize. Pressure decreases as movement improves. The system becomes more efficient. What once required intense force now moves more freely.

In life, something similar happens. When pathways form—habits of honesty, patterns of connection, rhythms of reflection—pressure becomes more manageable. Not because it disappears, but because it has somewhere to go.

Pressure without pathway feels crushing. Pressure with pathway feels purposeful.

This is why the path you couldn't see often becomes the path you wouldn't trade. Not because it was easy, but because it led somewhere real. Somewhere deep. Somewhere true.

People often look back on their lives and identify seasons they would never want to repeat—but would never want to erase. Those seasons changed them. They redirected them. They revealed capacities they did not know they had.

The path was hidden, but it was forming.

This does not mean every painful season leads to obvious resolution. Some paths remain unfinished. Some fractures do not connect as we expect. Some outcomes remain unresolved. Formation is not transactional. It does not guarantee closure.

But formation does guarantee change.

We are not the same after pressure as we were before it. The question is not whether we change, but how.

Do we become more open or more guarded?
More connected or more isolated?
More honest or more performative?

These are directional choices.

The path you couldn't see is shaped by these choices, made repeatedly, under pressure, over time.

Eventually, something reaches the surface.

It may be wisdom.
It may be compassion.
It may be clarity.
It may be calling.

Whatever emerges, it is not accidental. It is the result of pathways formed beneath the surface—pathways shaped by response rather than relief.

This is why pressure is not the enemy of direction. It is the means by which direction is revealed.

You may not see where this season is leading. That does not mean it is leading nowhere. The absence of visibility does not imply the absence of purpose.

The formation is responding.
The fractures are connecting.
The pathway is forming.

You are already on the path—even if you couldn't see it when you started.

Chapter 8

Intertwined on Purpose**

There is a difference between connection by accident and connection by design.

Much of life feels accidental. We meet people unexpectedly, experience hardship without warning, and find ourselves in circumstances we did not choose. From the surface, these intersections appear random—moments colliding without coordination or intent. But beneath the surface, something more deliberate is often taking place.

Fractures do not merely coexist.
They intersect.

In the subsurface, fractures are influenced by stress fields, material properties, and existing structures. They do not spread aimlessly. They follow lines. They seek points of intersection. When fractures meet, they reinforce one another. They create continuity. They become pathways.

Connection is not incidental.
It is structural.

This truth reframes how we interpret the intersections of our lives. The moments when our pain overlaps with someone else's. The seasons when our questions echo another's doubts. The times when our story resonates with someone we never expected to understand us.

These intersections are not coincidences.
They are invitations.

Invitations to recognize that our fractures are not isolated defects, but points of contact. Places where understanding can flow. Where compassion can move in both directions. Where shared pressure becomes shared strength.

This challenges the way we often think about brokenness.

We tend to treat brokenness as something to be repaired privately before reentering community. We believe we must heal in isolation and return once we are whole. But healing rarely works that way. Wholeness is not achieved before connection; it is formed through it.

Fractures do not need to be hidden to be healed. They need to be connected.

This connection is not superficial. It does not come from shared interests or common success. It emerges from shared vulnerability. From the courage to acknowledge what hurts and the humility to let others see it.

Vulnerability is often misunderstood as weakness. But structurally, vulnerability is openness. It is the willingness to allow pressure to move rather than stagnate. It is the decision to remain permeable under strain.

Permeability is what makes flow possible.

When fractures intersect, pressure redistributes. No single fracture bears the full weight. Stress spreads across the network. The system becomes more resilient, not less.

Human communities function the same way.

When pain is shared, it is not diminished—but it is distributed. What was unbearable alone becomes survivable together. This does not eliminate suffering, but it prevents collapse.

This is why isolation is so dangerous under pressure. Isolated fractures concentrate stress. Over time, they widen uncontrollably. They weaken the structure. Connection prevents this concentration.

Connection stabilizes.

This does not mean every intersection is safe. Discernment matters. Not every listener understands. Not every space honors vulnerability. But the risk of connection does not negate its necessity.

Without intersection, fractures remain terminal. With intersection, fractures become transitional.

They lead somewhere.

This is where purpose emerges.

Purpose is not always discovered in solitude. Often, it is revealed through relationship. Through shared experience. Through mutual recognition. We begin to see that our pain has prepared us to understand someone else's. That our struggle has given us language for another's silence. That our fracture has positioned us to offer presence rather than answers.

Presence is powerful.

In a world quick to explain, presence listens.
In a world eager to fix, presence sits.
In a world that avoids discomfort, presence stays.

Presence requires connection. Connection requires openness. Openness requires courage.

Courage is not the absence of fear.
It is the decision to remain open despite it.

When fractures intertwine, something larger than individual healing begins to form. Networks emerge. Communities take shape. Cultures of honesty develop. These cultures are not built on perfection, but on shared humanity.

They are resilient because they are real.

This reality changes how we interpret our own fractures. We stop asking only how to heal and start asking how to connect. We recognize that our pain has positioned us within a larger story—not as a footnote, but as a contributor.

Contribution does not require resolution.
It requires presence.

We do not have to be healed to be helpful. We do not have to be whole to be valuable. Our fractures, when acknowledged, become points of access. They allow others to approach us without pretense.

Pretense isolates.
Honesty invites.

This invitation is often quiet. It shows up in conversations that go deeper than expected. In moments when someone recognizes themselves in our story. In shared silence that communicates more than words.

These moments matter.

They reinforce the truth that we are intertwined on purpose. That our lives are not parallel lines, but intersecting paths. That our fractures are not obstacles to connection, but catalysts for it.

This perspective reshapes community.

Community becomes less about similarity and more about solidarity. Less about agreement and more about accompaniment. We stop expecting others to fix us and start allowing them to walk with us.

Walking together changes pace. It slows us down. It forces attentiveness. It creates space for reflection. It allows formation to continue rather than rush toward resolution.

Resolution is not always the goal.
Faithfulness often is.

Faithfulness to remain present.
Faithfulness to remain open.
Faithfulness to remain connected.

These commitments form the backbone of resilient communities.

In the subsurface, once fractures intertwine and stabilize, flow increases. What was once trapped begins to move freely. Pressure equalizes. Energy is redirected.

In life, when fractures intertwine, something similar happens. Healing accelerates—not because pain disappears, but because it finds context. It becomes part of a larger narrative. It is no longer the whole story.

This does not minimize suffering. It situates it.

Suffering gains meaning when it serves connection.
Connection gains strength when it bears suffering.

This reciprocal relationship is not accidental. It reflects design.

We were not created to endure pressure alone. We were designed for shared load-bearing. For mutual support. For collective resilience.

When fractures intertwine, they fulfill that design.

This realization changes how we approach our own pain. Instead of hiding it, we consider where it might connect. Instead of sealing it, we discern how it might serve. Instead of resenting it, we ask what it is positioning us to offer.

These questions do not romanticize pain. They redeem it.

Redemption does not erase scars.
It gives them significance.

The significance of our fractures is not found solely in personal growth, but in relational impact. In the way our openness invites others to be honest. In the way our presence creates safety. In the way our story intersects with another's at just the right moment.

These moments are rarely dramatic. They are ordinary, quiet, and easily overlooked. But they are formative. They shape lives.

Intertwined fractures form the strongest pathways.

They create routes not just for individual healing, but for collective transformation. They allow communities to move through pressure without fragmenting. They enable growth that is sustainable because it is shared.

This is why isolation is not only painful, but counterproductive. It resists the very mechanism designed to carry us through pressure. It keeps fractures terminal instead of transitional.

Connection turns fractures into bridges.

Bridges carry weight.
They connect separate places.
They enable movement.

Your fractures are not dead ends.
They are intersections.

Intersections are where journeys change direction.

And when fractures intertwine, they do so on purpose—not by chance, not by accident, but by design that understands how pressure forms pathways.

Chapter 9

The Pipe Always Leads Up**

Every pathway has a direction.

In the subsurface, fractures do not exist for their own sake. They are not the goal. They are not the destination. They are the means by which something deeper is brought upward. No matter how complex the network becomes, no matter how far it extends horizontally, every productive fracture ultimately connects to one thing—the pipe.

And the pipe always leads to the surface.

This is the truth that ties everything together.

Pressure reveals fractures.
Fractures form pathways.
Pathways exist for flow.

But flow has a destination.

In life, pressure alone is not the point. Breaking alone is not the purpose. Connection alone is not the end. All of it is directional. All of it is moving toward something—or more accurately, *toward Someone*.

God is not found only at the beginning of the story, nor merely in the fractures along the way. God is the surface.

God is the destination.
God is where everything broken is meant to rise.

This is where faith anchors the metaphor.

Scripture does not present God as distant from pressure, nor as offended by fracture. Instead, He is revealed as the One who works *through* them—guiding, redeeming, and directing what would otherwise remain buried.

"He brought me up out of the pit, out of the miry clay;
He set my feet upon a rock, and made my steps secure."
— Psalm 40:2

Notice the movement.
Out of the pit.
Upward toward stability.

The pit is not the end. The surface is.

In oilfield terms, a formation may be five miles down, locked under pressure, unseen and inaccessible. But once the pathway connects to the pipe, everything changes. What was once trapped begins to move. Gravity is no longer the governing force—direction is.

Redemption works the same way.

God does not deny the depth.
He redeems it.

Throughout Scripture, the movement of God is consistently upward—not in altitude, but in restoration. From chaos to order. From bondage to freedom. From death to life. From hidden to revealed.

Jesus Himself frames faith this way:

"I am the way, and the truth, and the life."
— John 14:6

A *way* is a pathway.
A *truth* is what pressure reveals.
A *life* is what flows when the pathway is complete.

The way does not bypass suffering.
The truth does not deny fracture.
The life does not ignore pressure.

It redeems all three.

This is why Scripture never promises a pressure-free existence. Instead, it promises presence within pressure—and purpose beyond it.

"We are afflicted in every way, but not crushed;
perplexed, but not driven to despair;
struck down, but not destroyed."
— 2 Corinthians 4:8–9

Afflicted—but not crushed.
That is the language of formation, not failure.

Paul continues just a few verses later:

"For this light momentary affliction is preparing for us an eternal weight of glory beyond all comparison."
— 2 Corinthians 4:17

Preparing.
Not punishing.
Not abandoning.

Pressure is preparation.

This is the key distinction: God does not waste fractures.

Every crack, every loss, every disappointment—when surrendered—becomes part of a pathway. Not a pathway away from Him, but one that leads directly to Him.

"The Lord is near to the brokenhearted
and saves the crushed in spirit."
— Psalm 34:18

Near.
Not distant.
Not waiting at the surface impatiently.

He is present in the depth, guiding the fractures, orienting the pathways, ensuring that what breaks does not scatter—but converges.

This is where the myth of randomness collapses.

Your pain is not directionless.
Your suffering is not pointless.
Your fractures are not terminal.

They are being oriented.

In the formation, fractures that do not connect to the pipe produce nothing. They may exist, but they do not flow. Connection to the pipe is what gives them meaning. In life, connection to God is what gives pressure purpose.

Without Him, pain may still shape us—but without direction.
With Him, pain becomes part of redemption.

Jesus speaks directly to this invitation:

"Come to me, all who labor and are heavy laden, and I will give you rest."
— Matthew 11:28

Rest is not escape from depth.
Rest is arrival at the surface.

Notice that He does not say, *"Avoid burden."*
He says, *"Bring it."*

Bring the pressure.
Bring the fracture.
Bring the weight.

The pipe is open.

This is why the Christian story is not about avoiding suffering, but about resurrection. Not about sealing cracks, but about rising through them. Not about staying intact, but about being redeemed.

The cross itself is the ultimate fracture—pressure applied until breaking occurs. And yet, through that breaking, the greatest pathway was formed.

"Surely he has borne our griefs
and carried our sorrows."
— Isaiah 53:4

He carried them upward.

Resurrection is the surface moment of the gospel. It is the declaration that pressure does not get the final word. Death does not get the final word. Brokenness does not get the final word.

God does.

This does not mean every story resolves neatly in this life. Some formations continue producing long after initial connection. Some flow is gradual. Some remains hidden for a time. But direction is established the moment the pathway connects to God.

Upward is now inevitable.

"Being confident of this, that he who began a good work in you
will bring it to completion."
— Philippians 1:6

Completion is the surface.

You may still feel deep.
You may still feel fractured.
You may still feel under pressure.

But if the pathway leads to Him, the outcome is not in question.

The pipe always leads up.

Pressure revealed the fractures.
Fractures formed the pathways.
Pathways led to the pipe.
And the pipe leads to God.

That is the truth beneath the surface.

And nothing—no depth, no pressure, no breaking—can stop what God is bringing up.

Final Chapter

Where God Fractured Me**

This book has talked about pressure, fractures, pathways, and the surface—but none of it matters if it remains theoretical.

At some point, the language has to become personal.
At some point, the metaphor has to meet a life.

This is where mine does.

I grew up in the church. I knew who God was. I understood His power. I could recite the stories, the promises, the verses. Faith was familiar to me—so familiar that I confused knowing *about* God with walking *with* Him.

And slowly, quietly, I drifted.

I did not rebel loudly. I did not abandon belief outright. I simply shifted the center. I began living as a *good person* rather than a *godly one*. I did what seemed right to me. I made my own plans. I chased my own definition of success. God was still present in my language, but no longer central in my decisions.

I lived for me.

Along the way, there were fractures—small ones at first.

Moments of conviction.
Quiet nudges.
Restlessness I couldn't explain.
Questions that surfaced and were quickly buried.

These were micro fractures.

They were not dramatic. They did not disrupt my life. They simply invited me to look up—to reorient—to return. And each time, I ignored them. I sealed them. I told myself I was fine. That I had time. That I was still a good person.

But fractures that are denied do not disappear. They wait.

The longer I ignored those micro fractures, the farther I drifted. God did not move. I did. And eventually, the distance felt so great that returning seemed almost impossible. I did not know how to go back. I did not know where to start. I had lived without alignment for so long that the idea of surrender felt foreign.

That is when God used a macro fracture.

In the subsurface, macro fractures are different. They are not subtle. They are not easily ignored. They run long enough and deep enough to reach places nothing else can. They cut through resistance. They connect what has been sealed for years.

For me, that fracture was my mother's cancer.

It was not sudden. It was not quick. It was a six-year battle—marked by thousands of prayers, moments of hope, stretches of fear, and small victories that kept us believing. We prayed for healing. We prayed for time. We prayed for strength.

And through it all, my mother prayed something deeper.

Her prayer was not first for her own healing. Her prayer was this: *"Do whatever it takes to bring my children back to their faith."*

That prayer fractures me even now.

Because the truth is painful and holy at the same time.

God answered her prayer.

But for me, it required a macro fracture.

Watching someone you love suffer dismantles illusions quickly. Control evaporates. Self-sufficiency collapses. The narratives you built to support your independence cannot survive that kind of pressure.

I could not explain it away.
I could not manage it.
I could not outwork it.

The fracture ran deep.

And in that depth, I found myself face to face with God—not as a concept, not as a memory, but as a presence. Not accusing. Not distant. Waiting.

"Before I was afflicted I went astray,
but now I keep your word."
— *Psalm 119:67*

Affliction was not punishment.
It was alignment.

That is the truth we resist until we experience it ourselves.

God did not fracture me to destroy me.
He fractured me to reach me.

The macro fracture did what years of micro fractures could not—because I refused to listen to them. It cut through my self-direction. It united the smaller, ignored fractures into a single, undeniable pathway back to Him.

That pathway led up.

I wish I could say it did not take that much. I wish I could say I turned earlier. I wish I could say I listened when the fractures were small. But honesty matters more than comfort here.

For me, it took depth.
It took length.
It took pain I would never wish on anyone.

And this is where the call to action becomes clear.

I do not want that for you.

God is gracious enough to use macro fractures—but they are not His preference. He whispers long before He shouts. He nudges before He breaks. He invites before He interrupts.

"Today, if you hear his voice,
do not harden your hearts."
— *Hebrews 3:15*

Micro fractures are mercy.

They are moments of conviction.
Moments of restlessness.
Moments when something in you says, *This isn't it*.
Moments when comfort feels hollow and success feels thin.

Those moments are not interruptions.
They are invitations.

The tragedy is not fracture.
The tragedy is ignoring it.

Macro fractures exist to unite micro fractures—to gather what has been scattered and force alignment. They are not random. They are directional. But they come at a cost.

If you are reading this and feeling that quiet pressure—pay attention.

If something in you is stirring—listen.

If God has been knocking softly—open the door.

"Return to me, and I will return to you,"
says the Lord.
— *Malachi 3:7*

Return does not require perfection.
It requires honesty.

You do not have to wait until life collapses to turn back. You do not have to hit bottom to look up. You do not have to endure a macro fracture to find the surface.

Use the micro fractures.

Let them connect.
Let them guide you.
Let them form the pathway.

God is not asking you to clean yourself up before coming home. He is asking you to stop sealing what He is opening. To stop resisting what He is revealing. To stop running from the pressure that is trying to save you.

> "A broken and contrite heart, O God,
> you will not despise."
> — *Psalm 51:17*

Brokenness does not repel Him.
It draws Him near.

My prayer for you is simple and costly and hopeful all at once:

May you not need a macro fracture to return.

May you recognize the mercy hidden in discomfort.
May you see conviction as kindness.
May you understand that pressure is not rejection, but pursuit.

God is the surface.
God is the destination.
God is where every pathway is meant to lead.

The fractures—micro or macro—are not the end of the story. They are how the story turns upward.

The pipe is open.
The pathway is forming.
The surface is waiting.

Come home.

Made in the USA
Coppell, TX
19 January 2026